STECK-VAUGHN
PORTRAIT OF AM

Virginia

Kathleen Thompson

A Turner Book

RSVP

RAINTREE
STECK-VAUGHN
PUBLISHERS
The Steck-Vaughn Company

Austin, Texas

Virginia

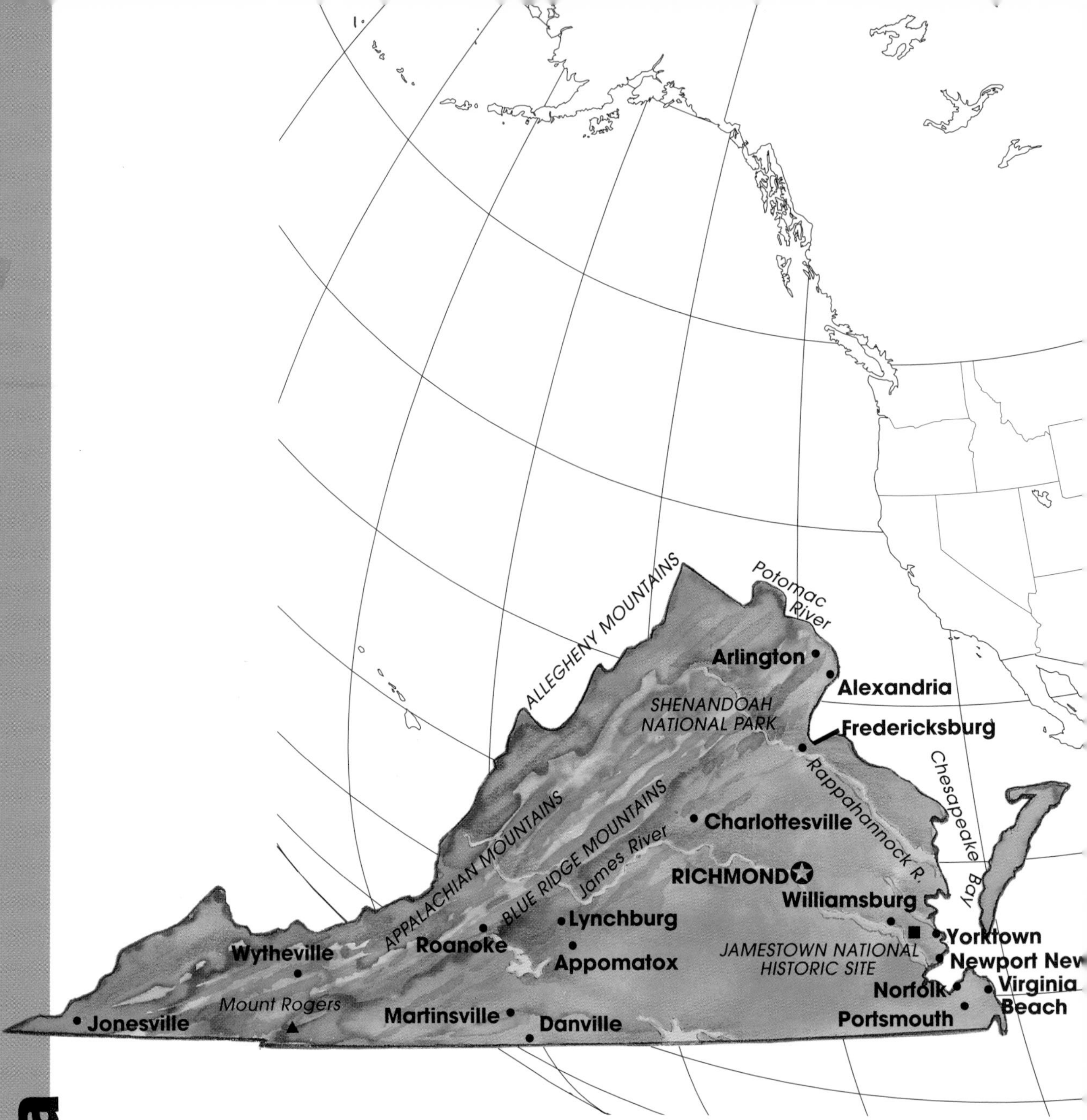

Arlington

Alexandria

Potomac River

SHENANDOAH NATIONAL PARK

ALLEGHENY MOUNTAINS

Fredericksburg

Rappahannock R.

Chesapeake Bay

Charlottesville

APPALACHIAN MOUNTAINS

BLUE RIDGE MOUNTAINS

James River

RICHMOND ⭐

Williamsburg

Lynchburg

Yorktown

Roanoke

Appomatox

JAMESTOWN NATIONAL HISTORIC SITE

Newport New

Wytheville

Norfolk

Virginia Beach

Mount Rogers ▲

Portsmouth

Jonesville

Martinsville

Danville

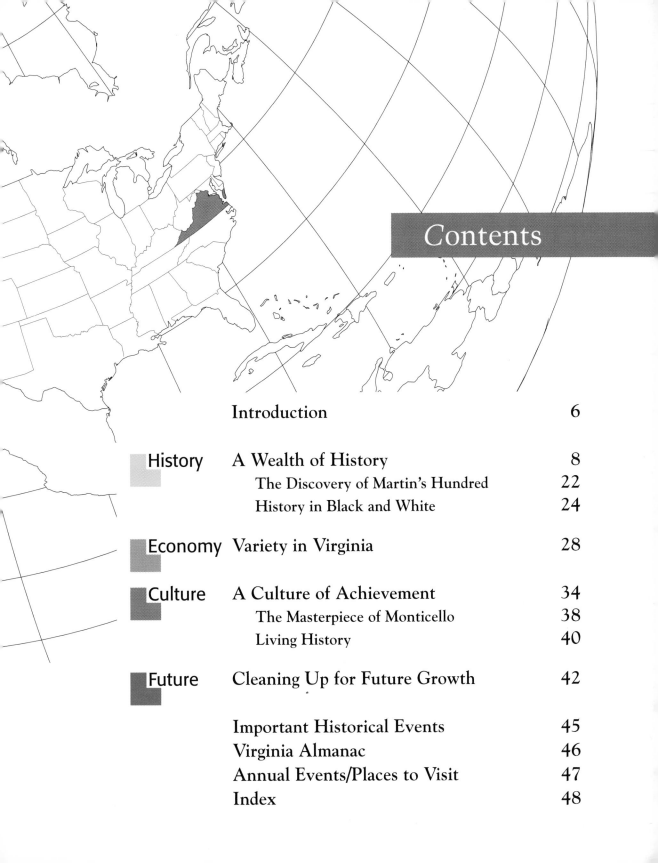

Contents

Introduction   6

History   A Wealth of History   8
               The Discovery of Martin's Hundred   22
               History in Black and White   24

Economy   Variety in Virginia   28

Culture   A Culture of Achievement   34
               The Masterpiece of Monticello   38
               Living History   40

Future   Cleaning Up for Future Growth   42

               Important Historical Events   45
               Virginia Almanac   46
               Annual Events/Places to Visit   47
               Index   48

Introduction

Perhaps no other state in the nation has contributed as much to our country's history as Virginia. Located midway down the Atlantic coastline, Virginia was the site of the first English settlement in the United States. Some of the most important battles of this nation's wars took place in this state as well. Virginia continued to be in the forefront of changes in this nation when it became the first state to elect an African American governor. Today Virginia plays an important national role in the federal government, in environmental protection, and in industry. The growth and changes that have refined Virginia throughout history also serve to illustrate the progress of our nation.

This farm is located in Virginia's fertile Shenandoah Valley. The valley spans more than 150 miles between the Blue Ridge Mountains and the Alleghenies.

Virginia

A Wealth of History

In the late fifteenth century, Native Americans living in the area of present-day Virginia comprised three powerful groups. The Powhatan were a branch of the Algonquin language group. They lived in the Tidewater region, near the ocean. The Powhatan were the largest and most powerful group in the region. The Monacan and the Manahoac, belonging to the Sioux language group, lived in the Piedmont Plateau region. The Susquehannock lived along the shores of Chesapeake Bay. Along with the Cherokee, they were a branch of the Iroquois. The Cherokee made their home in Virginia's southwestern mountains.

In 1584 England's Queen Elizabeth I sent Sir Walter Raleigh to colonize North America. He and a group of settlers arrived in present-day North Carolina in 1585, but by 1591 the colony had vanished. In 1606 King James I of England granted the land to the Virginia Company for the purpose of establishing plantations. In 1607 the Virginia Company's three ships arrived in today's Virginia with more than 100 settlers to start the colony.

This is a reconstruction of a Powhatan village. When the colonists arrived at Jamestown, there were 18,000 Native Americans living in the area.

This ship is a re-creation of the Godspeed, one of three ships that landed in Jamestown in 1607.

To pay respect to their king, the colonists called their new settlement Jamestown. The colony was built about 30 miles inland, on a marshy peninsula jutting out into the James River. It became the first permanent English settlement in North America. The location seemed ideal at first because the settlement was surrounded on three sides by water, making it safe from attack by Native Americans. Unfortunately the location turned out to be a poor choice. The land was low and swampy, the water was salty, and the air was filled

This painting depicts the construction of Fort James.

with mosquitoes. The poor conditions in Jamestown contributed to the failure of the settlers' crops. Many of the colonists became sick and died.

The Jamestown colony might have failed if it hadn't been for one strong leader. Captain John Smith organized healthy colonists into work parties. He went to the local Algonquin villages and traded goods, such as beads, cloth, and mirrors, for food. Some of the Native Americans were friendly and willing to trade. Others were not happy with the arrival of the newcomers. Powhatan, leader of the group of the same name and a chief of the Algonquin nation, ordered Smith killed. Smith was spared when Pocahontas, Powhatan's daughter, begged for his life. For a time there was an uneasy peace between the Algonquins and the colonists.

More colonists arrived at Jamestown in 1609. However, John Smith had to return to England after he was badly burned in a gunpowder explosion. The following winter of 1609–1610 was so bad that the settlers called it the Starving Time. About 435 of Jamestown's 500 people died of starvation or disease. The next spring, as the colonists were preparing to abandon Jamestown, a supply ship arrived, and the colony was saved.

In 1610 Jamestown was ruled by Lord Thomas West De La Warr and later by deputy governors Sir Thomas Gates and Sir Thomas Dale. The colony produced enough to continue year after year, but it did not flourish. By this time the population of Jamestown was about 700.

Pocahontas as a young Native American woman is depicted in this statue, which stands in Jamestown.

At Jamestown Settlement, costumed actors depict everyday life in the Jamestown colony. This man is splitting wood near a house built in the style of seventeenth-century colonial America.

In 1610 John Rolfe arrived and took over Smith's job of maintaining peaceful relations with the Native Americans. He had brought some tobacco seeds with him from the West Indies. When he saw the Algonquins growing tobacco, Rolfe decided his seeds might also do well in Virginia. Rolfe's crop flourished. The English couldn't get enough of the milder, high-quality Virginia tobacco. It now seemed that the colonists and the Virginia Company had found a way to make money.

In 1618 Sir Edwin Sandys took over the management of the Virginia Company. He divided the land into fifty-acre lots, which were granted to colonists who had worked the land for at least three years. Soon more and more land was cleared for planting tobacco. Some of the farmers became immensely rich from the profits on their crops, and they established huge farms called plantations.

Many of the early settlers in Jamestown were indentured servants. This was a system by which many poor Europeans had already traveled to Jamestown and other colonies. Indentured servants agreed to work for seven years without pay. Their employers paid for their passage. After the seven years, the servants were free to travel and work where they wanted. In 1619 the first Africans were brought to Jamestown by Dutch traders.

Between 1619 and 1622, about 3,500 people sailed to Virginia. Even with the added thousands arriving in the colony, Jamestown only had about 1,200 people by 1622. Contagious diseases took most of the colonists, and very few reached middle age. As Jamestown expanded, more and more land was taken away from the Native Americans. There might have been bitter fighting except that John Rolfe had married Pocahontas in 1614. Powhatan did not want to make war against his son-in-law's people. But Powhatan died in 1618. By that time, Rolfe, his young bride, and their small son had sailed to England, where Pocahontas died of smallpox. In 1622 Chief Opechancanough, who had replaced Powhatan, attacked the colonists. The Native Americans killed more than 350 settlers before they were driven back. The harsh winter of 1622–1623 brought another starving time. More than a hundred starved to death. In one year, the colony had lost almost half of its population.

Pocahontas changed her lifestyle and took the name Rebecca when she converted to Christianity and married John Rolfe in 1614.

The great number of deaths in Virginia angered King James I. In 1624 he dissolved the Virginia Company and made Virginia a royal colony. Royal governors were sent from England to rule. In 1634 Virginia's legislative body, the House of Burgesses, divided the colony into eight counties. Each county appointed a group of judges to maintain its own court of law and local government.

In 1649 the government of King Charles I, who succeeded James I, was overthrown, and the king was executed. For the next eleven years, England had no monarch. Oliver Cromwell, who led the revolt, ruled from 1653 until his death in 1658. During those years, Virginia ruled itself. Most of the colonists were still loyal to the Crown, however, and wanted to see the monarchy restored.

In England the supporters of the monarchy were called Cavaliers. Some fled to Virginia when Cromwell came to power. After Oliver Cromwell's death, Charles II, the son of King Charles I, regained control of England. He appointed William Berkeley as Virginia's new royal governor. Berkeley favored the Cavaliers over the original settlers. Once the Cavaliers had won seats in the legislature, he refused to call any new elections. This angered the settlers. Berkeley also refused to send troops to help defend new settlements against attacks by Native Americans. This also angered settlers.

In 1676 a young planter named Nathaniel Bacon, Jr. led a rebellion against Governor Berkeley. During the short-lived revolt, the rebels burned down Jamestown. The rebellion caught Charles II's attention, and in 1677 he removed Berkeley from office. As a result, Virginia farmers were given more seats in the House of Burgesses.

From about 1682, the economy of Virginia depended on the tobacco plantations. These were mostly in the coastal and south-central areas. The plantation owners used slaves from Africa to work the fields. About 350 families owned much of this land and held almost all the political positions.

Around the turn of the century some planters began moving farther west into the mountains. The French, who claimed the territory outside the colonies, objected strongly. The dispute helped lead to the French and Indian War, called this because many

Native Americans sided with the French against the British. During the war, a young Colonel George Washington led troops into battle. In 1763 the French surrendered. Great Britain acquired the former French territory east of the Mississippi and in Canada.

Great Britain wanted the colonies to help pay for the costs of the war. Starting in 1764, the British government imposed a series of taxes. The colonists objected to these taxes, especially since they were not asked for their approval. The colonists wanted to be represented in the government process that was taxing them.

In 1765, Patrick Henry, Thomas Jefferson, and other Virginians declared that only Virginia's legislature had the right to tax the people of Virginia. People who opposed "taxation without representation" were known as patriots. In 1773 some patriots from Boston dumped a shipload of tea into Boston Harbor to protest a tax on tea. Great Britain passed a law to punish the protesters. Virginia's House of Burgesses supported the Boston patriots, however, which caused the royal governor to dissolve the House of Burgesses.

In 1774 the First Continental Congress met in Philadelphia. Virginians Thomas Jefferson, Patrick Henry, and George Washington were among the delegates. The following year Virginians met in a convention and voted for independence from Great Britain. Patrick Henry made his famous plea for independence, saying, "Give me liberty or give me death." When the Second Continental Congress met in Philadelphia,

Delegates of the First Continental Congress sought George Washington's advice on military matters.

15

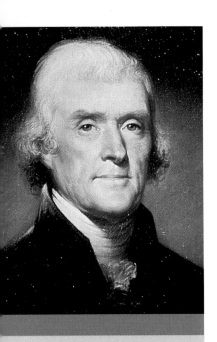

Thomas Jefferson was elected to two terms as President of the United States. At different times he also served his country as Vice President, secretary of state, congressman, and minister to France.

Pennsylvania, George Washington was appointed as commander-in-chief of the colonial army.

In June 1776 Virginia adopted its first constitution. The constitution included a Declaration of Rights written by George Mason. On July 4, 1776, members of the Second Continental Congress signed the Declaration of Independence, which was written by Thomas Jefferson.

Few Revolutionary War battles took place in Virginia. Perhaps the most important battle, however, was the last battle of the war. General George Washington trapped British General Charles Cornwallis at Yorktown, Virginia, in October 1781, and Cornwallis surrendered, ending the war.

Four years after the Treaty of Paris was signed in 1783, 55 representatives from 12 of the 13 states gathered to write a constitution for the new nation. Virginian James Madison, later called the "Father of the Constitution," led the effort. Each state had to approve the Constitution to join the Union. The Virginia delegates wanted to be sure their rights would remain protected. Virginia insisted that the new constitution carry the Declaration of Rights George Mason had written for Virginia's constitution. This proposal was rejected, but a Bill of Rights was added to the Constitution in 1791. Virginia approved the Constitution on June 25, 1788 and became the tenth state in the new United States.

Four of the first five Presidents of the United States were Virginians—George Washington, Thomas Jefferson, James Madison, and James Monroe. John

Marshall, the Chief Justice of the Supreme Court from 1801 to 1835, was also a Virginian.

All this glory and great civic contribution came from a state that was increasingly troubled, however. Virginia's economy was in decline because too much tobacco-growing had depleted the soil's nutrients. Also, high taxes reduced profits on agriculture. Eastern county plantation owners were still in control of the legislature, and western counties were demanding that the right to vote be given to all citizens, not just property owners.

The western counties also wanted the slaves to be freed. The matter received further attention after a Virginia slave named Nat Turner attempted a slave rebellion in 1831. The resolution to end slavery was brought up again in the Virginia legislature, but the bill was defeated.

The slavery issue was further dramatized in 1859 when John Brown and 22 other abolitionists seized the federal armory at Harpers Ferry, Virginia. Brown wanted to arm the slaves and then lead them in a rebellion. The plan did not work, and Brown was defeated by forces led by Colonel Robert E. Lee.

Besides slavery, another main issue leading up to the Civil War was states' rights. Southern states did not want the federal government dictating certain laws to them, especially concerning slavery. The South depended on slavery for its agricultural economy. The northern states wanted to abolish slavery and maintain a strong federal government. Abraham Lincoln, who became President of the United States in 1861, felt the

James Madison, the Father of the Constitution, was President during the War of 1812.

National harmony was the cornerstone of James Monroe's two terms as President.

same way many northerners did. Without much hope for immediate change, seven southern states withdrew from the Union. Virginia refused to join them. When Lincoln called for troops to fight the rebels, four more states, including Virginia, withdrew. Several of Virginia's northwestern counties did not follow the rest of the state. In 1863 they became the state of West Virginia.

During the Civil War, Virginia was the center of military and political operations for the Confederacy. Its capital, Richmond, became the Confederate capital. At the Battle of Bull Run in 1861, General Thomas Jackson, a Virginian, helped defeat the Union Army and earned the nickname "Stonewall." The following year Union General George B. McClellan moved his army up the York Peninsula toward Richmond. Along the way his troops took Yorktown, but McClellan's army was turned back by the army led by General Robert E. Lee. Also in 1862, Lee defeated Union forces at the second Battle of Bull Run, but was himself forced to fall back after the battle of Antietam, Maryland, one of the bloodiest battles in the war.

Lee defeated Union forces at Manassas in August 1862 and again at Chancellorsville the following May. Other important battles took place in Virginia at Fredericksburg, Wilderness,

General Robert E. Lee struggled with the decision to fight against the Union in the Civil War. However, he could not bring himself to fight against his fellow Virginians, who were members of the Confederacy.

Spotsylvania, and Cold Harbor. Finally, Union forces defeated Lee at Petersburg and Five Forks. General Lee surrendered at Appomattox, in central Virginia, in 1865.

The years after the Civil War were difficult for Virginia. The state had been heavily damaged by the

This photo, taken soon after the war, shows a burned-out section of Richmond. During the war, Richmond residents burned part of the city themselves, so that it would be of no use to the victorious Union Army.

fighting. Richmond was largely burned. The state also had a debt of about $47 million, although one quarter of this debt was eventually assigned to West Virginia. A new state constitution adopted in 1869 gave freed slaves voting rights and provided for a public school system. In the following years, however, blacks in Virginia lost many of the rights they had gained, and a system of segregation developed.

In the late 1800s, Virginia's economy improved. Coal fields opened up in southwestern Virginia. Railroads were extended throughout the state, improving shipping and transportation. The tobacco industry recovered, and other crops were added. Factories making cloth, furniture, and cigarettes were built.

During the 1920s more than 400,000 people left the state. Most of them were looking for better jobs. In the 1930s the country suffered under the Great

The battleship Mississippi leaves the shipyard at Newport News in 1917, ready to fight in World War I.

Depression. Millions of people were out of work, and banks and factories closed. Federal programs were created to bring more jobs into Virginia. When the country became involved in World War II in 1941, Virginia's economy received a boost. Factories built weapons, and shipyards launched aircraft carriers and fighting ships.

In 1954 the United States Supreme Court ruled that segregation of students according to their race in public schools was unconstitutional. In 1956 the Virginia legislature passed laws that closed any public school that the federal courts said had to be integrated. In 1959 those laws were ruled invalid by the courts. Even so, many parents kept their children from attending integrated schools. They sent them to private schools or taught them at home.

By the mid-1960s, most Virginia citizens had given up the fight against integration. In 1967 William F. Reid became the first African American to be elected to the state legislature since 1891. In 1989 Virginians elected L. Douglas Wilder governor. He was the first African American elected governor in any state.

In 1995 a number of Virginia rivers overflowed their banks as heavy rainstorms pounded the state for several days. The estimated flood damage reached one hundred million dollars.

Throughout its history, Virginia has produced war heroes and brave rebels. Now its leadership role has changed. Virginia's leaders are charged with setting good examples for its citizens and helping them to care for—and cope with—their environment.

above. During the late 1950s and early 1960s in Virginia, marchers of all races protested busing as a way to achieve school integration.

below. L. Douglas Wilder is interviewed by the press during his successful campaign to become governor of Virginia. Wilder was Virginia's governor from 1990 to 1994.

The Discovery of Martin's Hundred

British archaeologist Ivor Noël Hume was near Williamsburg, Virginia, in 1970 supervising a "dig," or archaeological excavation, along the James River. He was searching for artifacts at Carter's Grove plantation, which dates back to about 1715. What he found was much more interesting—a number of very old postholes.

"We took off the top layer of soil," Hume explains. "Underneath we found holes. In some of these holes we found the remains of posts. These indicate where fences, walls, and buildings once stood."

Hume's discovery of those post-holes was the start of a decade-long project that unearthed one of the earliest British settlements in North America. It was a colony called Martin's Hundred, and it only existed for about three years before it was destroyed. So far, it is the oldest British colony for which remains have been found. Jamestown is older, but the site of the original Fort James has never been discovered.

In 1618 a London group called Martin's Hundred prepared to send 220 settlers to America. No one knows for sure who Martin was, but he may have been Richard Martin, London's Recorder of Deeds in 1618. Whoever Martin was, he gathered one hundred

This photograph of Martin's Hundred shows the site from above. At the upper right, a group of workers are excavating artifacts.

This Native American village was reconstructed at a site near the original Jamestown. These houses, called wigwams, have a wooden framework, which is covered with bark, reeds, or woven mats.

investors to finance the voyage to Virginia. In 1618 people felt they could get rich by financing colonization. In addition, the first tobacco harvest from Jamestown had already reached London and was commanding premium prices. The prospect of large tobacco profits could easily have attracted one hundred investors.

Additional settlers arrived in Virginia in 1619 and immediately set about building a fort and town. However, the Native Americans had grown increasingly angry at the settlers for taking over so much land. On March 22, 1622, Native Americans attacked and killed 347 colonists and burned everything they could. At the Martin's Hundred settlement, 78 of the 140 settlers who remained were killed. Everything was burned except two

houses and part of a church. The remaining colonists tried to rebuild, but it was no use. By 1630 everyone had abandoned the former settlement.

"I think this is one of the most exciting archaeological projects ever done in this part of Virginia," Hume said. At Martin's Hundred, he found artifacts that show how people lived around 1620. He has discovered cookware, pieces of clothing, coins, weapons, and even a tobacco pipe. These silent items speak loudly of the brave people who crossed an ocean to find a new home nearly four hundred years ago.

History in Black and White

Virginia is a state rich in history. From Jamestown to the Revolutionary War to the Civil War and beyond, African Americans have been a vital part of the state's history.

Before the Civil War, there was enormous tension among the states concerning the issue of slavery. There was even more pressure in many areas of the South, including Virginia, where slaves worked on cotton and tobacco plantations. Because slaves greatly outnumbered the plantation owners, many plantation owners feared slaves would attempt an uprising.

In 1800 it almost happened in Virginia. A Richmond slave named Gabriel gathered a thousand slaves who were ready to rebel. Their attempt was defeated only by a thunderstorm that put off an attack. Word of the rebellion leaked out, and before Gabriel could regroup his army, the militia was called out. The rebels were defeated, and Gabriel and 34 of his followers were hanged. The fact that such a rebellion could even be planned frightened the plantation owners. Virginia governor James Monroe, later a United States President, commented that slave-holders could no longer "count with certainty on the tranquil submission" of the slaves.

Owning slaves was common in Virginia and throughout the South. Even George Washington (second from right) owned some slaves.

Nat Turner, another Virginia slave, tried leading a rebellion in 1831. He was a young preacher who believed that God had chosen him personally to lead the slaves out of bondage. He and his seventy-five followers killed about sixty landowners during a few days of bloody fighting. Turner was defeated, and about twenty of his rebels were hanged. What was worse, more than a hundred African Americans who had nothing to do with the rebellion were killed by terrified mobs.

Both slave uprisings showed the country that slavery could not go on forever. They also gave strength and pride to generations of Virginia's African Americans. In later years, another kind of rebellion was fought. It was a rebellion against laws that tried to keep African Americans from improving their lives.

In the 1850s, Margaret Douglass's four-room schoolhouse was the first school for free African Americans in the United States. Free African

Margaret Douglass's four-room school-house was the first school in the nation to teach former slaves.

Americans were former slaves who had been set free by their owners or had been allowed to buy their freedom. Even though these people were no longer slaves, they could not vote, own property, or seek an education. Margaret Douglass's school violated a Virginia law that banned "the instruction of all colored persons by means of books or printed papers." Douglass was thrown into jail for teaching African Americans to read and write.

The authorities could imprison Douglass, but they could not persuade her that what she had done was wrong. Later, looking back on the experience, she wrote these words: "I am happy to say, although I was afterwards cruelly cast into prison and otherwise unjustly dealt with, I have the satisfaction of knowing that I suffered in a good and righteous cause."

When the Civil War was over, and the slaves were free, things didn't automatically get better for African Americans. The former slave owners did everything they could to keep African Americans from attaining equality. But in Virginia, as in all the southern states, some outstanding people overcame the odds against them.

Booker T. Washington was born in 1856 in a one-room house with a dirt floor and no windows. He was a slave the first nine years of his life and didn't begin school until he was 12 years old. Washington worked five hours in the mines before school and went back to

Booker T. Washington was an ardent champion of education as a way for African Americans to achieve equality. Here he speaks at a political rally.

work after school. When he heard of the Hampton Institute, a school that would admit African Americans, he walked five hundred miles to Hampton to attend. Later, Washington became president of Tuskegee Institute, an outstanding trade school for African Americans. He also advised Presidents Theodore Roosevelt and William Howard Taft on race relations.

John Mercer Langston was another success. He was the first African American from Virginia ever elected to Congress. He also served as the foreign minister to Haiti. Langston was the first president of the Virginia Normal and Collegiate Institute, now Virginia State University, and dean of Howard University Law School.

Maggie L. Walker showed that African American women could achieve even at a time when gender made it even harder. In 1903 Walker became the nation's first female African American bank president.

Virginia's most recent African American success story came in 1989, when L. Douglas Wilder was elected governor of Virginia. He was the first African American governor of any state in the history of the nation.

In 1889 Booker T. Washington said, "No race can prosper till it learns that there is as much dignity in tilling a field as in writing a poem."

Virginia is a state that is proud of its history. Virginians can point to many famous people and glorious deeds. Virginia's history includes the deeds of many lesser-known people, too. These courageous men and women struggled and succeeded against great odds to ensure a future for Virginia's African Americans.

Variety in Virginia

Modern-day Virginia has a good mix of agriculture, manufacturing, and service industries to support its financial needs. The effect of this economic variety is evident. From the Civil War through the 1950s, Virginia remained one of the nation's poorest states. Per person income stayed well below the national average. In 1964 the General Assembly reduced business taxes to attract more industry. The response has been slow but steady. In twenty years, Virginia had just about reached the national average. Today Virginia ranks fifteenth in the nation in personal income and eight in average household income.

Virginia generates more than three quarters of its income from service industries. These are businesses that don't produce an actual product. Instead, they offer services to individuals and to other businesses.

In Virginia, government operations dominate the service sector. The largest single employer in Virginia is the United States government. That is because Washington, D.C., is just across the Potomac River.

Historic towns, such as Williamsburg, attract millions of tourists to Virginia. Tourism contributes nearly ten billion dollars to Virginia's economy every year.

One fifth of Virginia's workforce is employed by the state and federal governments. Many Virginians work in the Pentagon, which is the world's largest office building.

Many offices of the federal government, such as the Pentagon, are located in Virginia. Virginia is also home to many military bases. The Norfolk Naval Base is one of the largest navy base in the world. Quantico is a major training facility for the Marine Corps. The Army, Coast Guard, and the National Aeronautics and Space Administration (NASA) also have large facilities in Virginia. State and local government offices employ thousands of Virginians.

Virginia's service sector also consists of community, social, and personal services. These services include auto repair shops, doctors' offices, and engineering firms. In Virginia, many computer programmers, engineers, and research scientists do a great deal of their business with the federal government.

Next in importance are banking, insurance, and real estate services. Wholesale and retail trade follow. Wholesale trade involves selling goods in bulk, usually to retail stores. Retail trade consists of selling goods to individuals. A good example is supermarkets, which buy wholesale from suppliers and then sell retail to individuals. Transportation, communications, and utilities are also important services.

Manufacturing is also important to Virginia's economy. Chemicals are the most important product category. The South has traditionally been a major textile producer. Today, many of those textiles are synthetic fibers, such as nylon and polyester. These fibers are products of chemical plants. Medicines are also included among Virginia's chemical products.

Transportation equipment ranks third among manufactured goods. One of the world's largest ship-building and ship-repairing yard in the world is in Newport News. Virginia has other important shipyards in Norfolk, and Portsmouth. In recent years, Virginia has benefited from the shift of automakers and auto-parts makers to the southeastern states. Today, Virginia has almost sixty vehicle and equipment manufacturing facilities. It also has assembly facilities, such as the Volvo/GM heavy truck-assembly plant in Dublin. Aerialscope, a Richmond company, makes many of the fire trucks used by fire departments across the United States.

Food processing makes up the fourth largest area of

For nearly a century, Newport News shipyards have built some of the largest ships in the world. Here the aircraft carrier Theodore Roosevelt is launched.

Virginia is one of the leading states in turkey production. Next Thanksgiving, one of these birds might be on your dining room table.

manufacturing. Factories in Virginia process meat and shellfish. They also produce peanut butter, candy, beverages, canned and frozen foods, and bakery products. Another large area of manufacturing is electric machinery and equipment. Much of this is communications equipment.

Agriculture has become less critical to Virginia's economy than it was in the past. While still important, agriculture produces less than one percent of the state's income. Most of this comes from livestock and livestock products. In order of value, these are beef cattle, dairy products, chickens, and turkeys. Virginia is one of the nation's leading turkey-raising states. Hog farmers produce famous smoked Virginia hams.

Tobacco still is the most valuable crop in Virginia. Farmers also raise corn, hay, peanuts, soybeans, sweet potatoes, and tomatoes. Many large apple orchards can be found in the Shenandoah Valley.

Virginia is one of the nation's top coal producers. Most of the coal is bituminous, or soft coal, which is in less demand than it was twenty years ago. Burning soft coal causes air pollution, and recent laws have limited its use. Virginia also has limestone, granite, soapstone, and basalt quarries.

Fishing contributes about $90 million per year to the Virginia

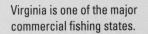

Virginia is one of the major commercial fishing states.

Soft coal is Virginia's most important mineral resource.

economy. The state is a leading producer of crabs, oysters, clams, and scallops.

One additional aspect of Virginia's economy is tourism. This growing industry contributes greatly to the state's financial picture. Virginia has a number of attractions to offer visitors. The Atlantic seashore on the east and the Blue Ridge and Allegheny mountains on the west are areas of great natural beauty. Virginia Beach is a leading East Coast resort town. State and national forests, as well as Shenandoah National Park, offer thousands of acres for wilderness getaways.

Visitors can also tour the homes of George Washington and Thomas Jefferson, as well as the restored colonial towns Williamsburg and Jamestown.

Clearly, Virginia has come a long way from its one-product economy—tobacco. Virginia's status as a state that works is something all Virginians can point to with pride and satisfaction.

White-water rafting on the James River is one of the many outdoor activities that brings tourists to Virginia.

A Culture of Achievement

Over nearly four centuries, Virginia has produced a great number of cultural achievements. Some have had a worldwide effect, such as the writings and speeches of Virginians at the time leading to our nation's freedom. Virginians were among the first Americans to call for independence. They also wrote the Declaration of Independence, contributed to the Bill of Rights, and helped write the Constitution.

Today their words still ring in our minds and hearts: "All men are created equal." "Governments derive their powers from the consent of the governed." "Congress shall make no law that shall abridge the freedom of speech or of the press." What writer could hope for a more glorious result than to contribute to the laws that shape the United States of America?

Virginia has produced its share of literary writers, too. Edgar Allan Poe lived and worked in Richmond for many years during the first half of the nineteenth century. He was a highly inventive writer. His story "The Murders in the Rue Morgue" is considered by

Jamestown Settlement is a living history museum. The park includes rebuilt colonial Williamsburg, where people in authentic costumes create original folk art.

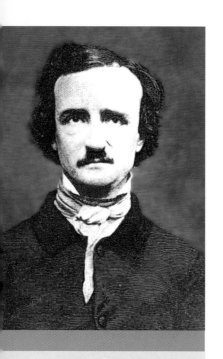

Although he was not born there, Edgar Allan Poe always referred to himself as a Virginian.

many to be among the first detective stories. Poe perfected the psychological thriller with "The Tell-Tale Heart" and other stories. He is also well-known as a poet, creating a number of lyrical poems such as "The Raven" and "The Bells."

Virginia's tradition of art includes the performing arts as well. One famous example is the Barter Theatre. During the Great Depression, a group of actors from New York City decided to find a rural place where they could barter, or trade, their performances for farm goods. They settled in Abingdon, a tiny town deep in the mountains of southwestern Virginia. For 14 years, the two dozen actors lived in an abandoned school and ate the apples, hams, vegetables, and other food that had been traded for performance passes.

In 1946 the Virginia legislature voted to give the Barter Theatre money every year to help it survive. The Barter Theatre was the first state-supported theater in the nation, and it became Virginia's state theater.

Part of Virginia's culture comes from products created by people living in the mountain regions. The art that they create has a more practical function than is common with many art forms. For example, these people play music for their own enjoyment and build and make things for their own use. Many of their songs and stories, as well as their handiwork, can be traced back to the seventeenth century. That is when northern Europeans immigrated to the United States and settled in the Appalachian Mountains and surrounding hills. Many of these people still weave cloth, make quilts, and build handmade furniture.

Many of Virginia's cultural items are showcased in more than two hundred fine museums. The Virginia Museum of Fine Arts, in Richmond, was the first state-supported art museum in the United States. Also in Richmond are the Science Museum of Virginia and numerous historic homes of colonial architecture. The Mariners' Museum in Newport News has exhibits that trace the history of ocean travel and commerce around the world.

Perhaps it should be expected that a state at the forefront of history would produce such a long-lasting culture. Virginia's culture has not lasted only because it is associated with our nation's history, however. Its cultural elements are unique and practical, and they were created to serve a need. Each has its own special history.

above. The Barter Theatre building, in Abingdon, was built in 1830 and originally was a church.

below. The Virginia Museum of Fine Arts sponsors dramatic and musical presentations, as well as popular touring art exhibits.

The Masterpiece of Monticello

Thomas Jefferson is perhaps best known for shaping the policies of the United States in its early days. He was the author of the Declaration of Independence, a document that still stands as the symbol of American freedom. He also advanced the influence of this country while serving two terms as the third President of the United States.

Thomas Jefferson was far more than a politician, however. He was without a doubt one of the most brilliant and widely accomplished men who ever lived. Jefferson was also a draftsperson, an architect, a surveyor, an astronomer, a naturalist, and a philosopher. In addition, he read seven languages, including ancient Greek and Latin, designed furniture and tableware, and played the violin.

Virginia abounds with proof of his talent. For example, Jefferson designed the state capitol building at Richmond. He also founded the University of Virginia. Then he surveyed the land for the campus and designed its buildings.

However, perhaps Jefferson's greatest legacy is Monticello, the 21-room home he built for his own use. Situated on a hilltop in central Virginia, not far from the scenic Blue Ridge Mountains, Monticello has been called one of the most beautiful homes in the United States. It is designed in a classic style, with white columns flanking the front entrance and a domed rotunda over the entrance hall.

Thomas Jefferson began building Monticello in 1769, when he was 26 years old. He continued to add to and remodel the building until the year before his death.

Monticello is considered to be one of the most beautiful colonial residences ever built.

Every room of the house holds artifacts that reveal Jefferson's many passions. In a windowed corner of one first-floor room is the telescope he used to study the stars. The library contains about 7000 books. A set of drafting instruments are arranged on one of his desks. The home also contains many pieces of furniture designed by Jefferson.

The gardens around the house show another side of Jefferson's genius. He loved plants, and gardening was a passion. Jefferson was continually trying to develop new and better varieties of fruits and vegetables. And, like any scientist, he kept accurate and detailed notes of each step, so he could repeat his results. In addition to his edible plants, Jefferson planted ornamental flower beds and many varieties of trees around Monticello.

Jefferson died at Monticello on July 4, 1826, fifty years to the day after the Declaration of Independence was signed. He was buried on his land in the Virginia hills he loved so deeply, near the house that has become a monument to his genius.

Living History

The history of Virginia has always been a vital part of the people who live there. Some people feel such a strong relationship with Virginia's past that they strive to relive it through reenactments of historical events. Attending a reenactment is like taking a step back in time. The sights and sounds of the battlefield are vividly brought to life. Nearby, campfires burn, and the smell of cooking food drifts over from the soldiers' encampment.

Recreating the past is a labor of love for participants in reenactments.

Participants spend hours researching details that will provide authenticity to a particular period of Virginia history. Some study battles that took place during the Revolutionary War or Civil War. Others research and re-create living in colonial Jamestown or Williamsburg.

The preparation for a historical reenactment is always thorough. Participants take great care to ensure that their clothing and equipment accurately reflect the time period. Sometimes participants will take on the role of a particular person who lived during that time period, such as a general, a color-bearer, a drummer, or

Civil War enthusiasts reenact a march into battle.

A Civil War battle is reenacted. Civil War forces usually lost 25 percent of their soldiers in every battle, because of death, injury, and capture.

a soldier. Others recreate the look and lifestyle of a colonial merchant, an innkeeper, a printer, or a blacksmith.

Sometimes reenactments take place at the same location where an event occurred. One year, spectators watched as the 1864 Battle of Trevilian Station from the Civil War was reenacted. In that battle, the Union's calvary forces under the command of General George Armstrong Custer faced off against the Confederates led by General Fitzhugh Lee. As the battle was reenacted, spectators watched soldiers mounted on horseback capture supply wagons as the battle raged on. To ensure safety, spectators were not allowed on the battlefield. However, they were allowed to walk around the army camps. They learned about what the soldiers ate and drank, where they slept, and what they did to prepare for battle.

Several thousand spectators watched as more than eight thousand people took part in this reenactment. Although many were Virginians, other participants came from all over the country. Whatever the historical subject, the bond that is shared by participants and spectators alike is the love of history and the desire to keep it alive.

Cleaning Up for Future Growth

As the state moves into the twenty-first century, Virginians can reflect on many changes that have occurred in the state. Certainly, one of the major changes has been an improved economy. Another is a recent surge in population growth.

Today, Virginia is growing rapidly, especially the northern part of the state. This is mainly due to the number of jobs available. Also, people are attracted to Virginia's pleasant natural surroundings. Some counties have tripled their population in the last twenty years. In some cases this growth has robbed the area of its natural beauty as expansion creeps into surrounding rural areas.

When people and industry are concentrated in any one area, pollution often becomes a problem. In Virginia, a certain amount of industrial waste is washed into the rivers. Farmlands have contributed to the problem, too. The fertilizers that are used to increase crop yields run off into water sources and join the other pollutants.

Virginia's future is dependent on the leadership it receives from Richmond, the state's capital and its most important industrial center.

This scene of downtown Norfolk looking across the James River shows the result of modernization and planning in Virginia's second-largest city.

Throughout most of Virginia, the rivers run eastward. They start in the western mountains and cross the state. Although Virginia is a coastal state, very little of Virginia's coast is open to the Atlantic Ocean. Instead, it borders a narrow finger of water, the three-hundred-mile-long Chesapeake Bay. This body of water receives most of the state's runoff pollution. Virginia's rivers are not the only ones that empty into the bay, however. The waters from many rivers eventually reach Chesapeake Bay. It is no wonder that the Chesapeake Bay is losing the fight to stay clean.

However, the states and cities that border the Chesapeake Bay are starting to fight back. Virginia, Maryland, Pennsylvania, and Washington, D.C., are investing millions of dollars in cleanup and educational efforts. For example, farmers are shown how to grow crops using less fertilizer. Research is under way to help factories clean their waste water.

Population growth is a natural result of a healthy economy. Virginians want to enjoy growth without harming the environment. Today's efforts will be a mark of how much more will need to be done.

Important Historical Events

1606 King James I of England forms the Virginia Company to colonize America.

1607 Jamestown becomes the first permanent English settlement in North America.

1610 More than eighty percent of the Jamestown settlers die from a lack of provisions.

1612 John Rolfe begins cultivating tobacco in Jamestown.

1618 Sir Edwin Sandys takes over management of the Virginia Company.

1619 The House of Burgesses is created.

1622 Chief Opechancanough attacks the Jamestown colonists, killing 347.

1624 Virginia becomes a royal colony.

1634 The House of Burgesses divides the colony into eight counties.

1676 Nathaniel Bacon Jr. leads a group of discontented colonists in a rebellion against the governor.

1693 The College of William and Mary is founded in Williamsburg.

1699 The capital is moved to Williamsburg.

1775 George Washington is made commander-in-chief of the Continental Army.

1776 The Declaration of Independence is signed. Patrick Henry becomes governor of the Virginia Commonwealth.

1780 The state capital is moved to Richmond.

1781 General Charles Cornwallis surrenders to General George Washington at Yorktown.

1788 Virginia becomes the tenth state.

1789 George Washington is elected the first President of the United States.

1792 Kentucky is created from the western counties of Virginia.

1801 Virginian John Marshall is appointed Chief Justice of the United States Supreme Court.

1831 Slaves led by rebel Nat Turner.

1859 John Brown leads an abolitionist raid on the federal arsenal in Harpers Ferry.

1861 Virginia withdraws from the Union. Richmond becomes the Confederate capital.

1862 The battle of the Monitor and the Merrimack (Virginia) is fought at Hampton Roads.

1863 West Virginia is created from Virginia's northwestern counties.

1865 General Robert E. Lee surrenders to Ulysses S. Grant at Appomattox.

1870 Virginia is readmitted to the Union.

1959 Public schools in Arlington and Norfolk are the first in Virginia to desegregrate.

1964 The 17-mile-long Chesapeake Bay Bridge-Tunnel is completed.

1967 William F. Reid becomes the first African American to be elected to the state legislature since 1891.

1969 A. Linwood Holton, Jr., is the first Republican to be elected governor in Virginia since 1869.

1970 Voters adopt a new state constitution.

1989 Virginians elect L. Douglas Wilder as governor. He is the first African American elected governor of any state.

1995 Heavy rains cause many of Virginia's rivers to overflow, causing millions of dollars in property damage.

The state flag of Virginia is dark blue. In the center is the state seal. It portrays a woman dressed as a warrior, holding a spear. She represents Virtue. She has one foot resting on the slain body of an enemy, which represents Tyranny. The state motto appears below.

Virginia Almanac

Nickname. Old Dominion

Capital. Richmond

State Bird. Cardinal

State Flower. Flowering dogwood

State Tree. Flowering dogwood

State Motto. *Sic Semper Tyrannis* (Thus Always to Tyrants)

State Song *Emeritus.* "Carry Me Back to Old Virginia"

State Abbreviations. Va. (traditional); VA (postal)

Statehood. June 25, 1788, the 10th state

Government. Congress: U.S. senators, 2; U.S. representatives, 11. State Legislature: senators, 40; representatives, 100. Counties: 95

Area. 40,598 sq mi (105,149 sq km), 36th in size among the states

Greatest Distances. north/south, 201 mi (323 km); east/west, 462 mi (744 km). Coastline: 112 mi (180 km)

Elevation. Highest: Mount Rogers, 5,729 ft (1,746 m). Lowest: sea level

Population. 1990 Census: 6,216,568 (16% increase over 1980), 12th among the states. Density: 153 persons per sq mi (59 persons per sq km). Distribution: 69% urban, 31% rural. 1980 Census: 5,346,797

Economy. Manufacturing: chemicals, tobacco products, transportation equipment, food products, electrical machinery and equipment, paper products, furniture, clothing. Agriculture: beef cattle, dairy cattle, chickens, turkeys, hogs, tobacco, corn, hay, peanuts, soybeans, potatoes, sweet potatoes, tomatoes, apples. Fishing: crabs, oysters, clams, scallops. Mining: coal, limestone, granite, basalt, clay, sand, gravel

State Seal

State Bird: Cardinal

State Flower: Flowering dogwood

Annual Events

★ Highland County Maple Sugar Festival in Monterey (March)

★ Dogwood Festival in Charlottesville (April)

★ Shenandoah Apple Blossom Festival in Winchester (May)

★ Harborfest in Norfolk (June)

★ Jazz Festival in Hampton (June)

★ Chincoteague Annual Pony Swim and Auction (July)

★ Scottish Games and Gathering of the Clans in Alexandria (July)

★ Highland Arts and Crafts Festival in Abingdon (August)

★ Jousting Tournament at Natural Chimneys, Mount Solon (August)

★ Old Fiddlers' Convention in Galax (August)

★ Neptune Festival in Virginia Beach (September)

★ State Fair in Richmond (September/October)

Places to Visit

★ Appomattox Court House National Historic Park, near Appomattox

★ Arlington National Cemetery

★ Assateague Island National Seashore

★ Blue Ridge Parkway scenic drive in western Virginia

★ Carter's Grove Plantation, along the James River in Williamsburg

★ Colonial Williamsburg

★ Edgar Allan Poe Museum in Richmond

★ James Monroe Law and Memorial Library in Fredericksburg

★ Jamestown Settlement

★ Manassas National Battlefield Park

★ Monticello in Charlottesville

★ Mount Vernon, near Alexandria

★ Shenandoah National Park

★ White House of the Confederacy in Richmond

Index

Allegheny Mountains, 6, 33
Abingdon, 36, 37, 47
African Americans, 6, 12, 21, 24–27
agriculture, 6, 11, 12, 17, 29, 32, 43, 44, 46
Algonquin, 9, 11, 12, 13
Appalachian Mountains, 36
Bacon, Nathaniel, 14
Barter Theatre, 36, 37
Battle of Bull Run, 18, 19
Battle of Trevilian Station, 41
Berkeley, William, 14
Blue Ridge Mountains, 6, 33, 38
Brown, John, 17
Cavaliers, 14
Charles I, King, 13, 14
Charles II, King, 14
Cherokee, 9
Chesapeake Bay, 9, 44
Civil War, 17, 18–19, 24, 26, 40, 41
Confederacy, 18
Cornwallis, Charles, 16
Cromwell, Oliver, 13–14
Custer, George Armstrong, 41
Dale, Thomas, 11
De La Warr, Thomas West, 11
Declaration of Independence, 16, 35, 38, 39
Douglass, Margaret, 25–26
Dutch Traders, 12
education, 20, 21, 25–26, 27, 44
Elizabeth I, Queen, 9
England 6, 9, 10, 11, 12, 13–14, 15, 16, 22
environment, 6, 21, 43, 44
First Continental Congress, 15
Fort James, 10, 22
France, 14–15
French and Indian War, 14–15
Gabriel, 24
Gates, Thomas, 11
General Assembly, 29
Godspeed, 10
Great Depression, 21, 36
Hampton Institute, 27

Harpers Ferry, 17
Henry, Patrick, 15
House of Burgesses, 13, 14, 15
Howard University, 27
Hume, Ivor Noël, 22
indentured servants, 12
industry, 6, 20, 21, 30–33, 43, 46
Iroquois, 9
Jackson, Thomas "Stonewall," 18, 19
James I, King, 9, 13
James River, 10, 33, 44
Jamestown, 9, 10–13, 22, 23, 33, 40
Jamestown Settlement, 12, 35, 47
Jefferson, Thomas, 15, 16, 33, 38–39
Langston, John Mercer, 27
Lee, Fitzhugh, 41
Lee, Robert E., 17, 18–19
living history, 40–41
Madison, James, 16, 17
Manahoac, 9
manufacturing, 20, 21, 29, 30–32, 46
Marshall, John, 17
Martin's Hundred, 22–23
Mason, George, 16
McClellan, George B., 18
mining, 20, 32, 33, 46
Mississippi, Battleship, 20
Monacan, 9
Monroe, James, 16, 17, 24
Monticello, 38–39, 47
museums, 37
National Aeronautics and Space Administration (NASA), 30
Native Americans, 9, 10, 11, 12, 13, 14, 15, 23
Newport News, 31, 37
Norfolk, 31, 44
Norfolk Naval Base, 30
Opechancanough, Chief, 13
Pentagon, 30
plantations, 9, 12, 14, 17, 22, 24
Pocahontas, 11, 13
Poe, Edgar Allan, 35–36, 47

population, 11, 12–13, 20, 43, 44, 46
Powhatan, 11, 13
Powhatan, culture, 9, 11
Quantico, 30
Raleigh, Walter, 9
Reid, William F., 21
Revolutionary War, 16, 40
Richmond, 18, 19, 24, 37, 38, 43, 46, 47
Rolfe, John, 12, 13
Sandys, Edwin, 12
Second Continental Congress, 15–16
segregation, 20, 21
service industries, 29–30
settlers, 6, 9, 10, 11, 13, 14, 22–23
Shenandoah National Park, 33, 47
Shenandoah Valley, 6
Sioux, 9
slavery, 14, 17, 20, 24–26
Smith, John, 11, 12
states' rights, 17
Susquehannock, 9
taxes, 15, 17, 29
Theodore Roosevelt, Carrier, 31
tobacco, 12, 14, 17, 23, 24, 32, 33, 46
tourism, 29, 33
trade, 11, 12, 30
transportation, 20, 30, 31
Treaty of Paris, 16
Turner, Nat, 17, 25
Tuskegee Institute, 27
United States Bill of Rights, 16, 35
United States Constitution, 16, 35
University of Virginia, 38
Virginia Company, 9, 12, 13
Virginia State University, 27
voting rights, 17, 20
Walker, Maggie L., 27
Washington, Booker T., 26–27
Washington, George, 15, 16, 24, 33
Wilder, L. Douglas, 21, 27
Williamsburg, 29, 33, 35, 40, 47
World War I, 20
World War II, 21